Meridian

Raymond Gibson

Glass Lyre Press

Copyright © 2016 Raymond Gibson
Paperback ISBN: 978-1-941783-20-7

All rights reserved: except for the purpose of quoting brief passages for review, no part of this book may be reproduced or transmitted in any form or by any means, electronic or mechanical, including photocopying, recording, or by any information storage and retrieval system, without permission in writing from the publisher.

Cover art: Helenstock | Dreamstime.com
Design & layout: Steven Asmussen
Copyediting: Linda E. Kim
Author Photo: Raymond Gibson

Glass Lyre Press, LLC
P.O. Box 2693
Glenview, IL 60026

www.GlassLyrePress.com

*Tongues are a ford through time's river;
they lead us to our dead forebears,
but one cannot quite arrive home there
who still fears the deep waters.*

—Vladislav Illich-Svitych

Presence

you are /7
facts are /8
we knit /10
notes beget /21
we gave /22
nothing is /24
young love /35
you who /36
couldn't see /38

Findings

Horizon /13
Lines /14
Each /15
Mask /16
Fleeing /17
Sight /18
Further /19
Lost /20
Memories /27
Burn /28
Once /29
Black /30
Egg /31
Bear /32
Stars /33
Findings /34
Conclusion /41

PRESENCE

you are not here
and neither am I

here is between us

the where in wherefore
where from its else-

one silent letter to
mark whole from hole

words maps or nets

a space not uniform
a scale not fixed

and now is forever

this stage upon stage
escheloned as if stairs

books stacked to heaven
words our sole footing

now now and now

tracks on a blizzard
of paper we are

gaps and echo misheard

notes of two songs
playing both at once

a disunion of thought
vaguely webs us in

its trick of perspective

we've never met before
few have if ever

are hours ours then

we may yet meet
on words between us

how else come here
pages by one spine

turn roll unfurl finlike

tongues in the way
tongues are the way

this silent speech this

spoken silence of mass
a volume like water

sunbright in its weight
present but inured to

a shared air breathed

♦

facts are facets are
things in the act

the truth speaks softly

as time saying amber
to the enduring sap

words come and go
like leaves like men

we the tree remain

time branches and roots
cause or effect braids

all the reticulated knots

the nerves rewiring in
a vast wounded brain

constellated in the sum
of each groping thought

bent toward what light

what faint truth said
through its ringed echo

by its nested metaphors

listen the wind blows
clear petals of sky

while a twig writes
upon air beyond ours

that we must change

so many bells peal
but they aren't time

words are not truth

the leaf isn't autumn
but its painted sign

its absence isn't winter
but clocks' stray hands

set to truth's rhythm

a pendulum of moon
ratchets off the days

we aren't there yet

seeds of each other
at a different pace

facets of all masks
converging to a face

facts are times efface

♦

we knit this poem
like two long needles

a line's wave threads

I am the absence
of you vice versa

warp and woof hid
from either's notice till

we've sides to regard

a spun coin's sphere
we make a tragicomic

Janus laughing to tears

there cannot be I
without you such skins

demark us like shores
embroider a fractal lace

ink seeping into grain

as poem stitches through
us like bone buttons

blood threads its veins

dear reader I'm trapped
beating on the other

page's side as likewise
are you words say

this much nothing more

trace the labyrinth wall
circle to the entrance

spiraling in and back

there is no outside
nor within only sides

thin worn bare threads
all paring to transparency

a fabric of non-fabric

a figment's segments fray
into the knitted brow

a dreamer upon waking

rises through a mirrored
depth to surface breach

non-breadth chase the line
reader writer please find

me between these words

Horizon

I want something beautiful to listen to
while the clock eats my time

want the horizon though I'm walled
in my eyes
             to dream myself awake line by
wavering line I want to hold
the universe in seven billionth scale before you

LINES

a moiré of raindrops skeins the surface all
oilslick and rainbow
                        as time's one tide
sucks us toward the future
                                lines are the wind
made visible though all is lost and dissolves

ah the crown of water that explodes

Each

I can barely tell the days apart anymore
the week is a quick arpeggio

each page is a different date
yesterday torn out
tomorrow is blank and opaque

we had now always this way
time burns all books we are the marginalia

Mask

in the mirror of my own blood through
the mask of my skull
my hair my flag these fingers my ramparts

my seashell castle
                the wave rolls eternity
what art outlives this trickling must abandon me

Fleeing

what are you
fleeing by these circles this spiral

                                            self

what are you
chasing by these circles this spiral

                                            self

Sight

the doll held a candle where it peered inside
itself this longing
to be elsewhere is the only place
to stand
       walls or no walls
gone snowblind from staring at or through

them and back into the crazed porcelain of sight

Further

nothing further
at the edge one may step out an inch

and thereby enlarge the world as much
or leap to disappear
                       as I so very tempted now
                       entertain
words map minds   minds make words

Lost

every presence is an absence somewhere
I am here because I am not yet there

gone between quo vadis and ubi sunt

by turns both lost and found
in some fur-lined cave where senses blunt

every exit enters somewhere

Presence

notes beget the string
the tale recounts itself

secrets hate their secrecy

open eyes cannot help
but to look outward

locks rust buried jewelry
will feed grave robbers

language begs two play

at the utmost least
one alone in solitaire

tore pages from self

bequeathed a deck of
weeks to other selves

memory a leaf rustle's
fall a rootbound mind

must shatter its vessel

beyond flies and stars
mortal mortar and pestle

of daily grinding sun

some smoky thing lasts
even if only motes

a crystal lattice or
just its fragile pattern

recurrently etched in dust

life diamond hard breaks
every part speech was

meant for the broken

and the joined although
never the silent whole

the answers never ask
footfalls tread to paths

moons flood tides wax

rising arcs will decline
winds past come again

gifts further indebt us

guest and host derived
from the same word

home haunts its ruin
might has already been

we were they'll become

♦

we gave divided houses
child stand up anyway

hierarchy is no symmetry

learn when we're lying
and reweave the tapestry

you aren't our image
but rather our likeness

take part leaving's half

O semblance to assemble
split the difference between

our afterglow and absence

futures make echoes motifs
generations amplify a belief

our heirloom despair ill-fits
resist our eager silencing

here is whatever's insisted

contexts shift like desert
sand within the horizonless

we've no other referents

but ourselves in iterations
mirage ideal and shadow

sweep and pivot around
the mind's numberless dial

word must become bond

without trust we're lost
to bull-headed panic by

the forest of ourselves

why decorate a mausoleum
or deceive upon maps

why shun old travelers
why bequeath youth traps

poet curate life's museum

child mend this world
fell our crooked pillars

fight noise's roaring static

reconcile these ages for
threefold cords are not

easily broken though all
can break and shall

tame time's fierce cages

♦

nothing is more durable
than this striving to

make some firm shape

it outlives its attempts
to lovingly foster others

fragile house of skin
man created the distance

from here to anywhere

here is a hand
with a keyhole tattoo

over a closed eye

this glass ball that
feigns it's the globe

where does this key
go the dead asked

now here is nowhere

sphinx what was man
thought word and thing

going gone going on

star spindrift in dark
maelstrom void a chaos

fizzle of neurons' fuse
a clutched heart choking

as the lungs ejaculate

we're born we die
catching half of life

as in sidelong glances

if only we'd share
we'd make some sense

but the words break
under the sky's weight

and roads part ways

is nothing more durable
than this longing to

make some shape firm

let dung beetles have
their pyramids and misers

count coins we have
the endless book subtle

fire what time wrought

Memories

the flower is what it is

there are no saints or saviors
we are all fools on the same path
we send scouts ahead
                            and kill messengers
our memories as short as these trampled petals

Burn

let no man count himself free
while the handiwork of slaves exists

the great pyramids are no more
than dung beetles' mounds taken to
a perverse extremity
                        burn my ashes thrice
let my name be forgot
than carve such pain into flesh and echoes

Once

gold you shiny rock
washed with blood and sweat
                      you aren't worth
a mouthful of water in the desert

greed is a cannibal

and money the tatters of the map
                that once covered all the earth

Black

death with your sky-blue baby face
death with your old woman hands
death with your black mist of sleep

death with your birdcage ribs
death with your skin-lined coffin
and death with your cenotaph teeth

    I am the puppet who plays its strings

Egg

I am fighting this room this room is winning

I will haunt paper
                       what if a statue hatched
like an egg what if I tore through this page
I am finding a way

O time it smites me   I reify fiery in ink

Bear

this stage has no back it is a gallows it is the world

the crowd is frenzied and dreams offer no respite

to bear it you lift up one calm friend
        not to take your place as none can
                but for the sheer companionship

STARS

I want to shoot an arrow out of the universe

the sea has no memory
memory cannot hold the sea

what anchors kites to an empty upturned palm

corpsewax and the candlelight of stars

FINDINGS

blink sky turn earth
time is the distance between any of us

we are only here because the sleeper never wakes

horizon lines each mask fleeing sight further
lost memories burn once

as a moth lays eggs on a flame I give these words

Presence

young love dies for
one another old love

lives for one another

as mercy conquers from
within force can't last

who can harm waves
with any great effort

but pouring oil's balm

under the shed skins
the ashes petals what

self different from you

over the stars grinding
in their same sockets

more power less control
more words less chance

getting through to you

the space between us
already thick with veils

we part like curtains

should I keep trying
to meet you halfway

we'll never quite arrive
you must reach out

let self persuade itself

how one meets another
and two become one

then fashion a third

and the third becomes
one that seeks another

that's you that's me
that's us that's them

we've all been here

this page is hybrid
partway you part me

its primal Gordian knot

lying about a distance
between time's slight arc

tangential to these lines
and elsewhere a center

of eternity of ourselves

♦

you who have stood
stand and will stand

the same but changed

what falls in error
rises back up again

there isn't any I
there isn't any we

only a self between

self subsumed in other
and other within self

a hand's thenar web

glows against the sun
as light consumes us

fans of eyes shutting
to a peacock feather

and finger to philtrum

nothing is ever lost
should mankind live on

tread the sword's edge

parting then and then
where burnt books laugh

thought can't be burnt
nor memory be buried

how the sword-tip glints

iris dilates time constricts
direction lies supine while

a tunnel running forever

turns all that mattered
to so much afterbirth

wind breath and words
blood beat and rhythm

yawning out stretch out

upend reach back inward
mirror echo and refract

clear flames glass wings

raining sparks a birdsong
that swirls in-and-out of

its ever higher harmonies
severing off chaos's distaff

these fibers our realities

◆

couldn't see eye to
eye we were eyes

set inside one face

couldn't meet when we
never parted two halves

of a compass orbiting
a spiral chasing itself

a recursion a chirality

this center was our
outmost limit seeking it

we found a pole

a zenith or nadir
distracted by an axis

it was always equidistant
like the silent horizon

carrying us with us

we never leave here
astral sand our hands

sift this sown glass

is no more diminished
for its touching us

all circles and spheres
ringing like vast bells

that light ricochets from

we who are present
fixed points falling within

the steady falling world

imagine a circle with
infinite radius zero radius

there is no circumference
the center is everywhere

all's divided by nothing

couldn't you see eyes
house more facets here

nothing we gave dies

who are we not
to string this poem

the notes knit facts
you have stood for

love durable is undivided

Conclusion

you won't meet the end elsewhere it will be
something brought with you

                            nothing is ever complete

to see this room from the vantage of another
yet life is two rooms like an hourglass's retorts

hover mirrorbody   may arrows split each other

Acknowledgments

Lines 1-120 of "Presence" previously appeared in *SPECS* 6 as "Presence I-III."

About the Author

Raymond Gibson graduated from the Creative Writing MFA program at Florida Atlantic University. His verse can be found in *White Stag, Gravel, Rust+Moth,* and *HOOT.* He currently lives in his hometown of Hollywood, Florida.

Glass Lyre Press

exceptional works to replenish the spirit

Glass Lyre Press is an independent literary publisher interested in technically accomplished, stylistically distinct, and original work. Glass Lyre seeks diverse writers that possess a dynamic aesthetic and an ability to emotionally and intellectually engage a wide audience of readers.

Glass Lyre's vision is to connect the world through language and art. We hope to expand the scope of poetry and short fiction for the general reader through exceptionally well-written books, which evoke emotion, provide insight, and resonate with the human spirit.

> Poetry Collections
> Poetry Chapbooks
> Select Short & Flash Fiction
> Anthologies

www.GlassLyrePress.com

www.ingramcontent.com/pod-product-compliance
Lightning Source LLC
Chambersburg PA
CBHW021200080526
44588CB00008B/427